The Story of a Special Day
Volume 242

August 29

The 241ˢᵗ day of the year (242ⁿᵈ in leap years). There are 124 days remaining until the end of the year.

by Michael Dobson

Timespinner
Press

This book is also available in e-book form for Kindle, e-pub devices, and other formats from your favorite online booksellers.

For more information about the series, about us, or about your special day, please email us at editor@timespinnerpress.com.

Look for other volumes in *The Story of a Special Day*, coming often. See www.timespinnerpress.com for details and for the most recent information.

Table of Contents

For the definition of "O.S.," "N.S.," "CE," and "BCE" used with some dates , see the section "On Names and Dates."

Cover: Two US Air Force Academy cadets in a ceremony marking the anniversary of the September 11 terrorist attacks (Photo: Raymond McCoy, USAF). The US Air Force Academy opened August 19, 1958 — the **Event of the Day** and **Cover Story.**

Quote of the Day

"Your character is not tested on occasions of public scrutiny or acclaim. It is not tested in moments when the object of your actions is the regard of another. Your character is what you are to yourself, not what you pretend to be to yourself or others."

John McCain, US senator
born August 29, 1936

Today
in
History
August 29

The Moon of Sturgeon August, P. D. Beckwith

What Happened on August 29?

While some days of the year are more famous than others, every day of the year is filled with important, exciting, and unusual events, from religious awakenings to natural disasters, from wars to breakthroughs in technology, and from tragedy to triumph.

In this section, you'll learn about all the events that make August 29 important, including the special event that makes up our cover story or event of the day. Some events you may already know about, others may be new to you, but all of them are important parts of the history of the work.

Let's explore some of the reasons why August 29 is a very special day!

The Class of 1959 entered before the new campus was built

A new class of Air Force Academy cadets during their first reveille formation.
(Photo: Mike Kaplan, USAF)

Event of the Day/Cover Story
US Air Force Academy Opens (1958)

Each branch of United States military has a service academy, dedicated to training its officers[*]. In order of their establishment, they are the United States Military Academy (better known as West Point), the United States Naval Academy (which trains officer for both the Navy and the Marines), the United States Coast Guard Academy, the United States Merchant Marine Academy, and the newest of the academies, the United States Air Force Academy, located in Colorado Springs, Colorado.

It was not until after the end of the Second World War that the United States Air Force became a separate military service. (Previously, it was the US Army Air Force.) The National Security Act of 1947 created a separate Air Force, and the new service needed an academy to train the officer needed for its new role. Congress authorized the new academy in 1954. A commission worked on establishing a permanent location and on designing the educational program.

The 582 sites initially considered were quickly reduced to three: Alton, Illinois; Lake Geneva, Wisconsin; and the winning site, Colorado Springs, Colorado.

---

[*] The US military academies are among the finest schools in the nation, and appointments are highly sought after. If you or someone you know is interested in attending one of them, see my book *How to Get Into a Military Service Academy* (Rowman and Littlefield, 2015).

The new academy was designed by the firm of Skidmore, Owings, and Merrill, and it was situated on 18,500 acres located on the east side of the Rampart Range of the Rocky Mountains. The cadet area of the campus is 7,258 feet (2,212 meters) above sea level. Its most iconic building, shown on the cover, is the Cadet Chapel. The chapel and other buildings in the Cadet Area are designed in a modernist style, using aluminum on building exteriors to suggest the outer skin of an aircraft.

The new campus wasn't nearly ready by the time the first cadets entered, so the Class of 1959 (entered 1955) was housed in renovated World War II barracks at Lowry Air Force Base, Denver. Junior officers from the other services, took on the roles of upperclassmen. The dedication ceremony was broadcast live on national television.

The Class of 1959 established a number of traditions, including the Cadet Honor Code and the selection of the falcon as the Academy's mascot. Famed Hollywood director Cecil B. DeMille designed a parade uniform for the cadets.

On August 29, 1958, the new campus opened, and the entire wing of 1,145 cadets moved to the Colorado Springs site. They were commissioned on June 3, 1959.

In its relatively short existence, the Air Force Academy has produced 403 general officers, 39 astronauts, 2 combat aces, and many others, including famed US Airways pilot Chesley Sullenberger, who safely landed his crippled aircraft in the Hudson River, and is the subject of the 2016 film *Sully*.

The US Air Force demonstration team, the Thunderbirds, flies over Falcon Stadium for the US Air Force Academy Class of 2009 graduation. Note the cadet parade uniforms, designed by Cecil B. DeMille. (Photo: Dennis Rogers, USAF)

Ishi (Photo: Saxton T. Pope)

More August 29 Events

From the creation of great works of engineering and art, to devastating wars and natural disasters, thousands of years of history have left their mark on each and every day of the year. Here are some important events that occurred on August 29. (Illustrated items are shaded.)

1898 — The **Goodyear** Tire and Rubber Company is founded. It is named for Charles Goodyear, inventor of vulcanized rubber, and is known both for its tires and for the iconic Goodyear Blimp.

The Goodyear Blimp (Photo: Tequask, CC BY-SA 4.0)

1911 — Ishi, last of the indigenous Yahi people from what is now California, is captured at the age of 50 while foraging for meat. He is considered to be **the last Native American to make contact with European Americans.**

1944 — The **Slovak National Uprising** begins as 60,000 Slovak troops turn against the Nazis. *(Photo page 49.)*

1949 — The **Soviet Union tests its first atomic bomb,** *First Lightning* (Первая молния) at Semipalatinsk in what is know Kazakhstan. *(See International Day Against Nuclear Tests, page 47.)*

1965 — **Gemini V** splashes down after setting a world record for manned space mission duration.

Gemini V astronauts Charles Conrad (left) and Gordon Cooper (right), on the deck of the recovery aircraft carrier following splashdown

1966 — The Beatles perform their last concert before paying fans at Candlestick Park, San Francisco.

1982 — Chemical element number 109, **Meitnerium** (named for physicist Lise Meitner), is synthesized for the first time.

2005 — **Hurricane Katrina** makes landfall in Louisiana, triggering the most costly natural disaster in US history and devastating the city of New Orleans.

The Beatles (Photo: Ingen Uppgift)

Quote of the Day

"If you enter this world knowing you are loved and you leave this world knowing the same, then everything that happens in between can be dealt with."

Michael Jackson, entertainer
born August 29, 1958

Births
and
Deaths
August 29

Ingrid Bergman, actress. Ingrid Bergman was born August 29, 1915, and died August 29, 1982

Notable August 29 People

With the current world population at about seven billion people, on average about 19 million people also celebrate their birthdays on August 29 — and that isn't counting millions and millions who came before! No matter when you were born, you share your birthday with many special people whose accomplishments (and occasionally embarrassments) have been noted as part of history.

In this section, you'll meet fascinating people who share your birthday. They're organized by what they're famous for, and then in reverse chronological order from most recent to earliest. Those who are shown in photographs or artwork have a box around them. We don't have photos of everyone, so please forgive us if your favorite person is missing.

Some of these people you've heard of, others will be new to you, but they all make up an important part of the reason that August 29 is a truly special day!

John Locke, influential political philosopher, born August 29, 1632.
Portrait by Sir Godfrey Kneller

Who Was Born on August 29?

Business and Technology

Charles "Boss" Kettering, American inventor, engineer, and businessman; head of research at General Motors and founder of Delco; held 186 patents for developing the electric starting motor, leaded gasoline, and Freon. *(1876)*

Charles Kettering on the cover of *Time* magazine (1933)

Fashion and Food

Todd English, celebrity chef who hosted the cooking show Food Trip With Todd English; his Las Vegas P.U.B. restaurant was inducted into the Culinary Hall of Fame. *(1960)*

Mr. Blackwell, fashion critic and media personality known for creating the annual "Ten Worst Dressed Women List." *(1922)*

Government and Politics

Neil Gorsuch, appointed as associate justice of the US Supreme Court by Donald Trump. *(1967)*

James Brady, White House press secretary under US President Ronald Reagan; shot during the attempted assassination of Reagan and subsequently became an advocate of gun control. *(1936)*

John McCain, US senator and 2008 Republican candidate for President; Naval aviator and POW during the Vietnam War. *(1936)*

Literature and Poetry

Count Maurice Maeterlinck, Belgian symbolist writer awarded the 1911 Nobel Prize in Literature. *(1862)*

Oliver Wendell Holmes Sr., American physician and poet best known for his 1858 book *The Autocrat of the Breakfast Table;* his son Oliver Wendell Holmes Jr. became a US Supreme Court justice. *(1809)*

James Brady (Photo: William Fitz-Patrick)

John McCain

Military and Adventure

Chris Hadfield, astronaut who was the first Canadian to walk in space; served as commander of the International Space Station for a long-duration mission in 2013. *(1959)*

Music

Liam Payne, singer-songwriter best known as a member of the boy band One Direction. *(1993)*

Meshell Ndegeocello, singer-songwriter known for the hit songs "Wild Night" and "If That's Your Boyfriend (He Wasn't Last Night)." *(1968)*

Michael Jackson, singer-songwriter and dancer whose album *Thriller* is the best-selling album of all time; twice a member of the Rock and Roll Hall of Fame (once as a member of the Jackson 5), as well and the Songwriter Hall of Fame and the Dance Hall of Fame; named the Most Successful Entertainer of All Time by Guinness World Records. Best known hits include "Beat It," "Billie Jean," "Thriller," Bad," and many others. *(1958)*

Don Schlitz, country music songwriter and member of the Country Music Hall of Fame; hits include "The Gambler," "Forever and Ever, Amen," and "When You Say Nothing At All." *(1952)*

Dick Halligan, founding member of Blood, Sweat & Tears; won a Grammy for Best Instrumental Performance for their hit "Variations on a Theme y Erik Satie." *(1943)*

The Jackson 5 from their 1977 television variety show The Jacksons. From left bottom: Randy, Marlon, Tito, Jackie, and **Michael Jackson** (driving the motorcycle)

Charlie Parker on saxophone, with Tommy Potter, Miles Davis, Dizzy Gillespie, and Max Roach (Photo: William P. Gottlieb)

Jimmy C. Newman, Cajun singer-songwriter and long time star of the Grand Ole Opry; member of the Cajun Music Hall of Fame. *(1927)*

Dinah Washington, most popular black female recording artist of the 1950s; hits include "What a Diff'rence a Day Made," ."Baby (You've Got What It Takes," "A Rockin' Good Way (To Mess Around and Fall in Love," and "September in the Rain." Member of the Rock and Roll Hall of Fame and the Big Band and Jazz Hall of Fame. *(1924)*

Charlie Parker, jazz saxophonist and composer known as "Yardbird" or "Bird;" leading figure in the bebob jazz movement and member of the Grammy Hall of Fame. *(1920)*

Performing Arts

Lea Michele, actress and singer best known for playing Rachel on the television series *Glee* from 2009 to 2015. *(1986)*

Carla Gugino, actress known for the *Spy Kids* films, *Watchmen,* and *Night at the Museum,* and for the television series *Karen Sisco* and *Threshold.* *(1971)*

Rebecca De Mornay, actress known for roles in *Risky Business, Backdraft,* and *The Hand That Rocks the Cradle.* *(1959)*

Lenny Henry, British stand-up comedian best known for co-founding the charity Comic Relief. *(1958)*

Robin Leach, entertainment reporter best known as host of *Lifestyles of the Rich and Famous* and for the catchphrase "champagne wishes and caviar dreams." *(1941)*

Elliott Gould, actor whose best known films include Bob & Carol & Ted & Alice, M*A*S*H, and *Ocean's Eleven* and its sequels. *(1938)*

William Friedkin, filmmaker who won the Best Director Oscar for *The French Connection;* other films include *The Exorcist* and *To Live and Die in L.A..* *(1935)*

Charles Gray, actor who played the Criminologist in *The Rocky Horror Picture Show* and Blofeld in the Bond film *Diamonds Are Forever. (1928)*

Betty Lynn, actress best known for playing Barney Fife's girlfriend Thelma Lou on *The Andy Griffith Show. (1926)*

Richard Attenborough, director and producer of *Gandhi, A Chorus Line,* and *Chaplin;* actor in *The Great Escape, Flight of the Phoenix, The Sand Pebbles,* and *Jurassic Park. (1923)*

Isabel Sanford, actress best known for playing Louise "Weezy" Mills-Jefferson on the sitcoms *All in the Family* and *The Jeffersons. (1917)*

George Montgomery, actor and stuntman known for numerous Western film roles and the television series *Cimarron City. (1916)*

Elliott Gould

Isabel Sanford (right) with Sherman Hemsley in *The Jeffersons*

Ingrid Bergman, actress known for such films as *Casablanca, Notorious,* and *Gaslight;* won three Academy Awards; mother of actress Isabella Rossellini. *(1915[†])* *(Photo page 18.)*

Barry Sullivan, actor who appeared in over 100 films including *The Bad and the Beautiful, Payment on Demand,* and *A Life of Her Own. (1912)*

Preston Sturges, Academy Award-winning filmmaker best known for his screwball comedies, including *The Great McGinty, The Lady Eve, Sullivan's Travels, The Miracle of Morgan Creek,* and many others. *(1898)*

Philosophy and Religion

Charles Grandison Finney, Presbyterian leader during the Second Great Awakening religious movement in the United States, sometimes known as "the father of modern revivalism." *(1792)*

John Locke, influential political philosopher often called "the father of liberalism;" his ideas on government by the consent of the governed and the rights of life, liberty, and property are at the foundation of the US Declaration of Independence. *(1632) (Portrait page 20.)*

[†] Ingrid Bergman's date of birth and death are both August 29; she died on that date in 1982.

Science and Medicine

Stephen Wolfram, computer scientist and physicist who founded Wolfram Research and led the design of the program Mathematica and the Wolfram Alpha answer engine. *(1959)*

Temple Grandin, professor of animal science and autism spokesperson named by *Time* magazine to its list of the 100 most influential people in the world; subject of the 2010 biopic *Temple Grandin*. *(1947)*

Arthur B. McDonald, Canadian astrophysicist who shared the 2015 Nobel Prize in Physics for solving the solar neutrino problem by demonstrating that neutrinos have mass. *(1943)*

Otis Boykin, African-American inventor and engineer who held 28 patents, including a control unit for the artificial cardiac pacemaker. *(1920)*

Nathan Pritikin, nutritionist and longevity researcher best known for creating the Pritikin diet and exercise regime. *(1915)*

Sir John Charnley, British orthopedic surgeon who pioneered the hip replacement operation. *(1911)*

Vivien Thomas, pioneering African-American surgical technician who developed a treatment for "blue baby syndrome;" subject of the award-winning 2004 television film *Something the Lord Made*. *(1910)*

Werner Forßmann, shared the 1956 Nobel Prize in Physiology or Medicine for developing the procedure that allowed cardiac catheterization. *(1904)*

Social Activism

Henry Bergh, founded the American Society for the Prevention of Cruelty to Animals (ASPCA). *(1813)*

Sports

Roy Oswalt, baseball pitcher for the Houston Astros and other teams; three-time All Star and won a gold medal in the 2000 Summer Olympics as a member of Team USA. *(1977)*

Jerry D. Bailey, American Hall of Fame jockey who won 5,893 races with total purses of $296 million in a thirty year career, including winning each Triple Crown race twice. *(1957)*

Bob Beamon, American track and field athlete who won an Olympic gold medal in the 1968 games by breaking the world record in the long jump. *(1946)*

Wyomia Tyus, American track and field athlete who won three Olympic gold medals in two games; first person to retain the Olympic title in the 100m event. *(1945)*

Herb Simpson, Negro League baseball player with the Seattle Steelheads, the Birmingham Black Barons, and the Chicago American Giants. *(1920)*

Roy Oswalt (Photo: D. B. King, CC BY-SA 2.0)

Bob Beamon (Photo: Dutch National Archives, CC BY-SA 3.0)

Lee Marvin in *The Twilight Zone* episode "The Grave."
He died August 29, 1987

Who Died on August 29?

Art and Illustration

John Steuart Curry, painter known for his work in the American Regionalism style. *(1897)*

Business

Alfred Peet, entrepreneur who founded the Peet's Coffee & Tea company. *(2007)*

David T. Abercrombie, founded the lifestyle clothing brand Abercrombie & Fitch. *(1931)*

George Huntington Hartford, led The Great Atlantic and Pacific Tea Company (A&P) in the creation of the concept of the chain grocery store, and built A&P into the largest retailer in the US. *(1917)*

Crime and Punishment

Richard Jewell, security guard who discovered a pipe bomb during the 1996 Atlanta Olympic Games; falsely accused of planting the bomb himself but was eventually exonerated after an FBI investigation. *(2007)*

Libero Grassi, Sicilian clothing manufacturer killed by the Mafia for his public refusal to pay them protection money. *(1991)*

Nathan Leopold Jr., kidnapped and murdered a 14-year old boy in 1924 with fellow student Richard Loeb. The "Leopold and Loeb" story was considered "the crime of the century." Leopold and Loeb were defended by noted attorney Clarence Darrow, and were sentenced to life plus 99 years. *(1971)*

Richard Loeb (left) and **Nathan Leopold** (right) (Photo: ABC, Georg Pahl, 1924. Courtesy Bundesarchiv, CC BY-SA 3.0)

Government and Politics

Éamon de Valera, leader in the Irish War of Independence who subsequently led the introduction of the Irish constitution, served as president and taoiseach (prime minister) of that country. *(1975)*

Literature and Poetry

Gertrude Chandler Warner, American author of children's stories, most notably *The Boxcar Children* series. *(1979)*

William Archibald Spooner, absent-minded Oxford don known as the name sake of "spoonerisms," in which syllables of spoken phrases are mixed up for comic effect, such as "It is kisstomary to cuss the bride," "kinkering congs their titles take,"and "mardon me, padam, this pie is occupewed." *(1930)*

Caricature of **William A. Spooner**, by Leslie Ward (*Vanity Fair*)

Music

Honeyboy Edwards, Delta blues guitarist and singer whose life is featured in the 2010 film *Honeyboy and the History of the Blues;* awarded a Grammy Lifetime Achievement Award and named to the Blues Hall of Fame. *(2011)*

Lale Andersen, German singer-songwriter best known for her 1939 version of "Lili Marlene" which was popular among troops on both sides in the European theater of World War II. *(1972)*

Performing Arts

Gene Wilder, actor, director, and screenwriter known for *Blazing Saddles, Young Frankenstein, Willy Wonka & the Chocolate Factor, Silver Streak,* and *The Woman in Red. (2016)*

Shelagh Fraser, actress primarily known for playing Luke Skywalker's aunt in the first released film in the *Star Wars* series. *(2000)*

Frank Perry, director of films including *David and Lisa, The Swimmer, Diary of a Mad Housewife,* and *Mommie Dearest. (1995)*

Lee Marvin, actor known for his Academy Award-winning performance in 1965's Cat Ballou, and for roles in *The Man Who Shot Liberty Valance, Ship of Fools,* and *The Dirty Dozen. (1987) (Photo page 34.)*

Archie Campbell, comedian best known for the country television series *Hee Haw. (1987)*

Evelyn Ankers, actress and "scream queen" known as "Queen of the Bs" for her roles in numerous horror films, most notably *The Wolf Man, Son of Dracula,* and *Hold That Ghost. (1985)*

Sherlock Holmes and the Voice of Terror (1942). From left to right: Nigel Bruce, **Evelyn Ankers,** and Basil Rathbone

Ingrid Bergman, actress known for *Casablanca, Gaslight,* and Notorious, among other films. *(1982‡) (Photo page 18.)*

---

‡ Ingrid Bergman's date of birth and death are both August 29; she was born on this date in 1915.

Jean Hagen, actress nominated for a Best Supporting Actress Oscar for playing Lina Lamont in the 1952 film *Singin' in the Rain,* and for playing wife Margaret Williams in the 1950s television series *Make Room For Daddy. (1977)*

Jean Hagen

Religion

Brigham Young, second president of the Church of Jesus Christ of Latter-Day Saints (Mormon Church); known as the "American Moses" for leading the Mormon pioneers to the Salt Lake Valley; founded Salt Lake City and served as first governor of the Utah Territory. *(1877)*

Brigham Young (Photo: Charles William Carter)

Science and Technology

Pierre Lallement, French inventor who was the first to patent the pedal bicycle in the US. *(1891)*

Pierre Lallement

Sports and Games

Edmond Hoyle, writer best known for his books on the rules for card games; the phrase "according to Hoyle," meaning according to the best authority, refers to his expertise. *(1769)*

A SHORT

TREATISE

On the GAME of

Back-Gammon.

CONTAINING:

A TABLE of the thirty-fix Chances, with Directions how to find out the Odds of being hit, upon fingle, or double Dice.

Rules whereby a Beginner may, with due Attention to them, attain playing it well.

The feveral Stages for carrying your Men home, in order to lofe no Point.

How to find out who is forwardeft to win a Hit.

Cafes ftated for Back-Games, with Directions how to play for one.

Cafes ftated, how to know when you may have the better of faving a Gammon by running.

Variety of Cafes of Curiofity and Inftruction.

The Laws of the Game.

By *EDMOND HOYLE*, Gent.

DUBLIN:

Printed for GEORGE and ALEXANDER EWING, at the *Angel* and *Bible* in *Dame-Street.*

M DCC LIII.

Hoyle on Backgammon (1753)

Quote of the Day

"Happiness is good health and a bad memory."

Ingrid Bergman, actress
born August 29, 1915

Holidays Around the World
THER
AC~
MAGNA
August 29

Miner, by Boris Jeremejewitsch Wladimirskij — for **Ukrainian Miner's Day**

August 29 Events

If you're looking for a reason to take your special day off, you should know that every single day is a holiday somewhere in the world! Here's some of what you can celebrate on August 29!

General Events

Dzień Straży Gminnej (Poland)

Poland celebrates Municipal Police's Day on August 29.

Individual Rights Day (Objectivists)

Followers of Ayn Rand observe August 29, the birth date of John Locke, as Individual Rights Day.

International Day Against Nuclear Tests (Kazakhstan, United Nations)

The United Nations observes August 29, the day in 1949 that the Soviet Union exploded its first atomic bomb, as a day of awareness and education about the dangers of nuclear testing. The bomb was exploded at the Semipalatinsk Test Site, Kazakstan; the test site was closed August 29, 1991. *(See also page 13.)*

Miner's Day (Ukraine)

The nation of Ukraine honors its miners on August 29.

National Sarcoidosis Awareness Day (US)

Awareness and education of the disease of sarcoidosis is observed in the US on August 29 by Congressional joint resolution and Presidential proclamation.

National Sports Day (India)

India celebrates National Sports Day on August 29, the birthday of legendary hockey star Dhyan Chand, who won Olympic gold medals for India in the 1928, 1934, and 1936 games.

A statue of hockey legend Dhyan Chand in Jhansi, Uttar Pradesh (Photo: Work2win, CC BY-SA 3.0). Dhyan Chand's birthday is celebrated in India as **National Sports Day**

Telugu Language Day (India)

Telugu is one of six languages designated as a Classical Language of India, with 74 million native speakers. Telugu Language Day marks the birth of pioneering Telugu linguist Gidugu Venkata Ramamoorty, born August 29, 1863.

Výročie Slovenského Národného Povstania (Slovakia)

Slovak National Uprising Anniversary commemorates the August 29, 1944, uprising of Slovaks against Nazi Germany. *(See also page 14.)*

Slovak mutineer forces of the 18th Anti Aircraft Artillery Battery (Photo: Pavel Pelech) — for the **Slovak National Uprising Anniversary**

Food Days

In the United States, almost every day of the year is dedicated to a particular food. (Some other countries also have official food days, but only in America is there one every single day!) Sponsored by manufacturers, retailers, farmers, or simply fans, these days are often proclaimed by the President, Congress, state governors, or mayors. Given that there are more different foods than days of the year, some days honor more than one kind of food!

In the US, August 29 is **National Chop Suey Day.** While many people believe that chop suey was invented by Chinese American cooks working on the transcontinental railroad, it actually comes from a regional Chinese dish called *tsap seui* (杂碎), which translates as "miscellaneous leftovers."

Chop suey usually consists of meat and eggs cooked with bean sprouts, cabbage, and celery, with a thick sauce. It's usually served with rice, but when it's combined with stir-fried noodles it becomes chow mein. *(Photo: Daderot)*

While **National Whiskey Sour Day** is usually August 25, some people celebrate it on August 29 instead. Some celebrate it more often. Not coincidentally, its also **National Lemon Juice Day**, because lemon juice is an important ingredient in whiskey sours.

A whiskey sour cocktail — for **National Whiskey Sour Day** (Photo: Jgilgamesh, CC BY-SA 3.0)

If you're health conscious, August 29 is also **More Herbs, Less Salt Day**. Chop suey may have herbs, but usually has a lot of salt. Whiskey sours, you'll be glad to know, have neither.

Although no country has as many food holidays as the US, the last Sunday of August (which sometimes falls on August 29) is **National Burger Day** in the United Kingdom.

Food Months

In addition, the entire month of August is used to celebrate numerous foods. Here's a list of what to eat in the month of August!

- Family Meals Month
- Get Acquainted with Kiwi Fruit Month
- National Catfish Month
- National Dippin' Dots® Month
- National Goat Cheese Month
- National Panini Month
- National Peach Month
- National Sandwich Month

Jar of Peaches, by Claude Monet — for **National Peach Month**

Religious Feast Days and Holidays

Saint Days

Each day in the year is considered a feast day for one or more saints. They are somewhat different in western Christianity (Catholicism and many forms of Protestantism) and in eastern (Orthodox) Christianity.

In *Western Christianity*, August 29 is the feast day of Saints Adelphus of Metz, Eadwold of Cerne, Euphrasia Eluvathingal (Syro-Malabar Catholic Church), John Bunyan (Episcopal Church), and Sabina.

In *Eastern Orthodox Christianity*, it is also the commemoration of Saints Candida and Gelasia of Constantinople, Theodora of Thessaloniki, Arcadius of Arsinoe, Basil I the Macedonian, Euthymius, Saebbi of Essex, Medericus, Vellecius, and Alberic. (These saints are honored on August 16 by "Old Calendrists [§].")

Beheading of Saint John the Baptist

One of the oldest traditional feasts in Christianity is the commemoration of the beheading of St. John the Baptist. It is observed on August 29 in most Christian traditions, although "Old Calendrist" Orthodox churches observe it on September 11.

[§] "Old Calendrists" use the older Julian calendar for liturgical purposes rather than the modern Gregorian one. See "What Day of the Week is August 29?" for the differences between the Julian and Gregorian calendars.

According to the Synoptic Gospels, John the Baptist was imprisoned by Herod Antipas (son of the Biblical King Herod) because John had criticized Herod for marrying his niece Herodias. On Herod's birthday, Herodias' daughter Salome danced before the king and his guests. Her dancing pleased Herod so much that in his drunkenness he promised to give her anything she desired, up to half of his kingdom.

When Salome asked her mother what she should request, she was told to ask for the head of John the Baptist on a platter. Although Herod was appalled by the request, he reluctantly agreed and had John executed in the prison.

The Feast of Herod, by Peter Paul Rubens — for the observance of the **Beheading of John the Baptist**

Honorary Months and Moveable Celebrations

Presidents, Congresses, and nations around the world issue proclamations recognizing particular months to honor certain causes. If not otherwise specified, all months are US. Here are some honorary designations for August.

- American Adventures Month
- American Artists Appreciation Month
- American Indian Heritage Month
- Audio Appreciation Month
- Bystander Awareness Month
- Children's Eye Health and Safety Month
- Child Support Awareness Month
- Digestive Tract Paralysis (DTP) Month
- Get Ready for Kindergarten Month

A 1943 nursery school for women working in the war effort. (Photo: Marjory Collins) — for **Get Ready for Kindergarten Month**

- Month of Philippine Languages (Philippines)
- National Back to School Month
- National Black Business Month
- National Breastfeeding Month
- National Children's Vision and Learning Month
- National Immunization Awareness Month
- National Lawn Games Month
- National Minority Donor Awareness Month
- National Water Quality Month
- Neurosurgery Outreach Month
- Psoriasis Awareness Month
- Spinal Muscular Atrophy Awareness Month
- Tomboy Tools Month
- What Will Be Your Legacy Month
- Win with Civility Month

Moveable and Multi-Day Events

Some events take place over a specific week or time period. Some events occur on different days each year (such as "fourth Saturday of a month"). These events sometimes take place on or include August 29. All are US unless otherwise specified.

Movable Events

Last Sunday (August 25-31)

- National Grandparents Day (Taiwan)
- Pony Express Day

Last Monday (August 25-31)

- Father's Day (South Sudan)

- Heroes' Day (Philippines)
- Liberation Day (Hong Kong)
- Late Summer Bank Holiday (England, Northern Ireland and Wales)

Last Saturday (August 25-31)

- Franchise Appreciation Day

An 1860 advertisement for Pony Express riders — for **Pony Express Day**

Non-Gregorian Events

Not every culture uses the familiar Gregorian calendar, so some events not only shift within a range of a few days depending on the year, but may even migrate through the months. Here is a selection of events around the world that sometimes take place on August 29.

- Chaturmas (Hindu calendar, also observed in Jainism, Buddhism)
- Aadi Perukku (Tamil calendar, Hinduism)
- Ghanta Karna (Nepali calendar)
- Raksha Bandhan (Hindu calendar)
- Nag Panchami (Hindu calendar)
- Rosh Hashanah LaBehema (Judaism)
- Shravana Putrada Ekadashi (Hindu calendar)
- Jhulan Purnima (Hindu calendar)
- Onam (Malayalam Calendar, Hinduism)
- Varalakshmi Vratam (Hindu calendar)
- Kumbh Mela (Hindu calendar)
- Raksha Bandhan 2015: August 29 (Hindu calendar)
- Teejdi 3rd day of Raksha Bandhan (Hindu calendar)
- Gai Jatra (Nepali calendar)

Just for Fun

Anybody can make up a holiday, and many people do! While none of these are officially recognized and some may come and go, here are a few more holidays for August 29.

- According to Hoyle Day (birthday of Edmond Hoyle, expert on card game rules)
- Go Topless Day (Sunday closes to August 26)
- International Tongue Twister Day (last Saturday)
- Tug-of-War Day (last Wednesday)

Tug-of-War competition at the 1904 Olympic Games — for **Tug-of-War Day**

Quote of the Day

"Make haste slowly."

Augustus, first emperor of Rome
and namesake of the month of August

About
the
Month
of
THER
ACU
MAGNA
August

"August," from the *Brevarium Grimani* by Simon Bening (c.1510)

August: The Eighth Month

In the parching August wind,
Cornfields bow the head,
Sheltered in round valley depths,
On low hills outspread.
  — *"A Year's Windfalls," Christina G. Rossetti*

In ancient Rome, the month we know as August was originally known as *Sextilis*, meaning sixth. That's because the Roman calendar of the time had March as the first month of the year. It originally had only 29 days, but in his great calendar reform in 45 BCE, Julius Caesar added two days to the month. In 8 BCE, the month was renamed August in honor of Augustus, first emperor of Rome.

It's often claimed that Augustus stole one of February's days to add to his month, but the month already had 31 days long before Augustus became emperor. Augustus chose the month because it was the time of year in which he had accomplished some of his greatest triumphs, including the conquest of Egypt.

In both the Julian and Gregorian calendars, August is the eighth month of the year. It's one of seven months that have 31 days. During leap years, August and February start on the same day of the week; in non-leap years years, no month begins on the same day of the week as August. However, August and November always end on the same day of the week, regardless of the type of year.

In the Northern Hemisphere, August is a summer month, and in many European countries, the holiday month for most workers. In the Southern Hemisphere, August is the equivalent to February, deep in winter. No matter which hemisphere, August is a good month to spot a meteor; the Perseid Meteor Shower always takes place during the month.

August is also the month in the US that has the highest birthrate.

August in Other Cultures

The month of August has different names in different languages. Some nations use calendars other than the Gregorian, and their months may overlap with June. In lunar-based calendars, such as Islam, months move through the seasons. Still, many languages often have a word for August itself.

Albanian: Gusht

Arabic (Egypt, Sudan, Yemen): يونأغسطس (Aġustus)

Arabic (Levant): حزيراآب ('āb)

Arabic (Libya): الصهانيبال (hānībāl)

Arabic (Algeria and Tunisia): جوأوت (Ūt)

Arabic (Morocco): غشت (ġušt)

Azerbaijani: Avqust

Basque: Abuztu

Chinese: 八月 (Cantonese: baatyuht; Mandarin: bāyuè; Taiwanese: peh-goeh)

Croatian: Kolovoz

Czech: Srpen

Finnish: Elokuu

French: Août

German (Swiss): Auguscht (in other German dialects, it's just "August.")

Greek: Αύγουστος (Aúgoustos)

Hebrew: אוגוסט (âvgûst)

Hindi: अगस्त (agast)

Hungarian: Augusztus

Irish (Gaelic): Lúnasa mí Lúnasa

Italian: Agosto

Japanese (traditional calendar): 九月 (kugatsu), 長月 (nagatsuki)

Korean: 팔월 (palweol)

Lithuanian: Rugpjūtis

Maori: Hereturikōkā

Old English: Wēodmōnaþ

Polish: Sierpień

Russian: август (Avgust)

Sesotho: Phato

Spanish and Portuguese: Agosto

Swahili: Agosti

Thai: Singhakhom

Vietnamese: 腩伮 (tháng tám)

Welsh: Awst

Yiddish: אויגוסט (oygust)

Zulu: uAgasti

August Sayings and Superstitions

Here are some sayings and superstitions associated with the month of August.

General Supersitions

"Agosto, mês do desgosto," or "August, the month of sorrow and grief." (Brazil)

"If a cold August follows a hot July / It foretells a winter hard and dry." (Farming)

If thunderstorms occur in early August, they will continue for the rest of the month.

Don't sail on the second Monday in August, because it was the day the ancient kingdoms of Sodom and Gomorrah were destroyed. (Old seafaring superstition)

If you bathe at midnight on August 1 (Lammas Day) in Lockmaur, Sutherlandshire, you'll be cured of all bodily ailments, but you're expected to repay the Spirit of the Lake with coin. (Scotland)

Wedding Supersitions

"August, better have waited." (Western Kentucky)

"An August bride will be agreeable, And practical as well."

"Married in August's heat and drowse / Lover and friend in your chosen spouse."

"Whoever wed in August be, many a change is sure to see."

The following days in August are considered auspicious for weddings: August 2, 11, 18, 20 and 30.

As for which day of the week to get married, that's easy.

> Monday for health, Tuesday for wealth,
> Wednesday best of all, Thursday for losses,
> Friday for crosses, Saturday for no luck at all.

A Regency wedding proposal

August Symbols

Birthstone: Peridot or sardonyx.

Peridot

Sardonyx (The ancient Cup of the Ptolemies, probably made in Alexandria, Egypt, in the 1st Century CE)

Birth Flowers: Poppy or Gladiolus, both symbolizing strength of character, love, marriage, and family.

Vase with Cornflowers and Poppies, by Vincent van Gogh

Vase with Red Gladioli, by Vincent van Gogh

"August," by Eugène Grasset

  Michael Dobson

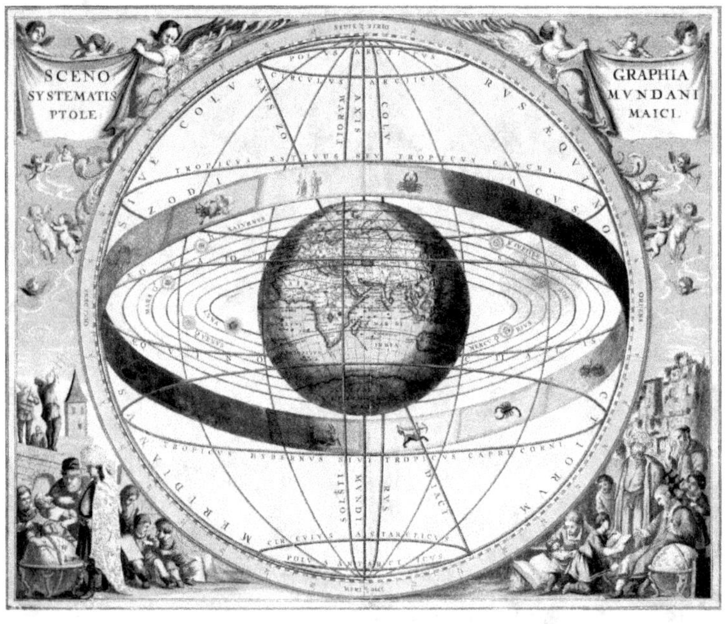

Scenography of the Ptolemaic Cosmography, by Johannes van Loon, based on Andreas Cellarius's *Harmonia Macrocosmica,* 1660

August 29 Zodiac Signs

From the perspective of someone on Earth, the Sun appears to move through the sky throughout the year, along a path astronomers call the *ecliptic plane*. The ecliptic plane is divided into twelve constellations, known as the zodiac, based on traditionally observed patterns of stars. On your birthday, you can't see your constellation, because it's in the daytime sky.

The zodiac was first developed by Babylonian astronomers about 2,500 years ago. Because they were unaware that the Earth wobbles like a spinning top (known as *precession*), they didn't make allowance for the fact that the Sun's path through the zodiac changes over time.

That means there are now two sets of dates for your birth sign. The *tropical dates* are the original Babylonian dates; the *sidereal dates* tell you where the Sun actually appears as it moves along its annual path.

For August 29, the tropical sign is **Virgo** and the sidereal sign is **Leo.**

Virgo

Tropical August 23 to September 23
Sidereal September 16 to October 15

The constellation of Virgo was originally associated with the grain harvest and symbolized fertility. The Greeks and Romans saw Virgo as Demeter or Ceres, the goddess of agriculture. In art, Virgo is often represented as carrying two sheaves of wheat. In the Middle Ages, Virgo was also sometimes connected to the Virgin Mary.

In astrology, Virgos are associated with being observant, helpful, and reliable, but can be perceived as inflexible and cold. They are supposed to be compatible with Taurus, Cancer, and Capricorn, but not with Gemini, Libra, or Aries.

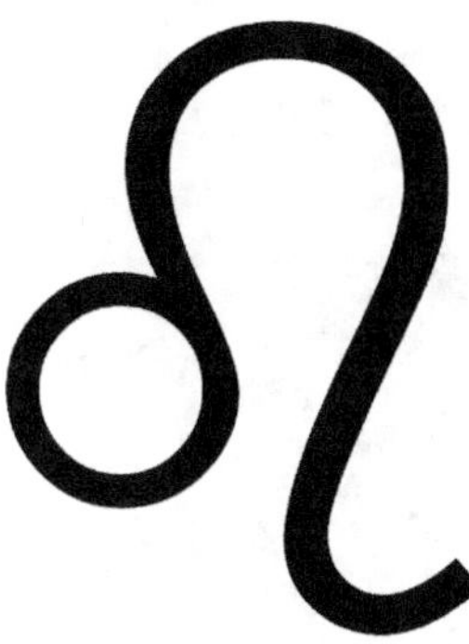

Leo

Tropical July 23 to August 22
Sidereal August 16 to September 15

Leo is one of the earliest recognizable constellations, with its stars forming a sickle or backward question mark. The Mesopotamians, the Persians, the Jews, and the Indians all had a name for the constellation that meant "lion." In Greek mythology, the Nemean lion was impervious to any weapons, but the hero Hercules nevertheless defeated it.

In astrology, Leo is a fire sign, suggesting that Leos are strong-willed and passionate. Leos are supposed to be compatible with Aquarius, Aries, and Sagittarius, but not with Gemini, Capricorn, or Pisces.

Illustration by Edward Penfield

What Day of the Week is August 29?

On what day of the week does August 29 fall?

Surprisingly, this isn't an easy question. Because the calendar year is 365 days long (366 in leap years), it doesn't divide evenly by the seven days of the week.

Also, the Earth goes around the Sun in about 365-1/4 days, so a calendar tends to drift over time. That's why the same date falls on different weekdays in different years.

This is made even more complicated by a change in calendars that took place in 1582. Our modern calendar has its roots in ancient Rome, in a calendar reform conducted by Julius Caesar. Caesar commissioned mathematicians to attack the problem, and they came up with the idea of leap years, and thus standardized the calendar for centuries to come. This was called the Julian calendar.

Over time, however, the small errors in Caesar's calculation compounded. That's why Pope Gregory XIII commissioned the Gregorian calendar, used in most of the world today. Some countries converted in 1582, when the calendar was first developed; some converted later; other still haven't changed.

Gregorian and Julian aren't the only types of calendars. The Hebrew year, the Islamic year, and many other calendars are used in different parts of the world and among different people.

You can convert Gregorian dates to other calendars, including the Hebrew calendar, the Islamic calendar, and even the Mayan calendar by visiting the Fourmilab Calendar Converter at http://www.fourmilab.ch/documents/calendar/.

Chinese calendar systems are quite complex and have changed several times; a full discussion is far beyond the scope of this book. If you're interested, you can find information here: http://www.hermetic.ch/cal_stud/chinese_cal.htm.

On Names and Dates

Historians use "CE" (Common Era) and "BCE" (Before the Common Era) instead of the more common "AD" (Anno Domini, or Year of Our Lord) and "BC" (Before Christ), reflecting the fact that the year-numbering system established by the Gregorian calendar is used throughout the world in many countries not culturally Christian.

The CE/BCE designation dates back to at least 1708, and has been adopted as a standard by the United Nations and the Universal Postal Union. Because this series of books covers events and people of all nations and cultures, we use the CE/BCE terms.

The abbreviation "O.S." ("Old Style") and "N.S." ("New Style") on some dates refers to the fact that the Russian Empire (in particular) did not switch from the Julian to the Gregorian calendar at the same time as the rest of Europe, and therefore some figures and events have two dates.

Also, in the Julian calendar in England in the 16th century, the year began on March 25 rather than January 1. To avoid confusion with Gregorian dates, dates between January and March were often written using both years.

People and events whose original names are not in the Western alphabet have their native names (where possible) in the appropriate script shown in parenthesis. If you are using an e-reader to access an electronic version of this book, all characters don't always display on all devices.

A 50-year brass perpetual calendar.

Quote of the Day

"Time is an illusion, lunchtime doubly so."

Douglas Adams,
from *The Hitchhiker's Guide to the Galaxy*

Notes
and
Credits
THE-R
ACC
MAGNA
Timespinner
Press

Cartoon by John T. McCutcheon

Copyright, Credit, and Contact

Follow Us

Our blog "This Day in History" (http:// timespinnerpress.com/this-day-in-history/) features short articles on events and people associated with each day, and updates several times each week. Also subscribe to the "Quote of the Day" at http://timespinnerpress.com/quote-of-the-day/. You can get daily links by following us on Facebook at TimespinnerPress, or on Twitter as @sidewisethinker.

Contact Us

Find an error or a format problem? Want information about the series, about us, or about when the volume for your special day might be available? Please email us at editor@timespinnerpress.com. (We also take requests if your special day isn't yet complete. Please give us at least six weeks' notice if possible.)

Sources

We owe a great debt to Wikipedia, which is our first stop for research. We attempt to make independent confirmation of all important dates and facts through a variety of other sources.

Other sources we frequently use include the Library of Congress; "on this day" listings from *Encyclopedia Britannica*, the *New York Times*, and the BBC; Omniglot for the names of months in other languages; *Chase's Calendar of Events*; and, of course, the always essential Google.

All art and photographs are either in the public domain, used under a Creative Commons license, or with a "fair use" justification, and most frequently come from Wikimedia Commons and the Library of Congress Prints and Photographs Division.

Attribution is provided where possible, or as requested by the copyright owner, or when there is particular historical significance, listed below. For information about any particular illustration or photograph, please contact us.

Credits

1. The cover photograph of the Air Force Academy Chapel used on the cover was taken by Carol M. Highsmith in 2007, and is from the Carol M. Highsmith's America Collection at the Library of Congress Prints and Photographs Division (digital ID highsm04090). According to the Library, Carol M. Highsmith has stipulated that her photographs are in the public domain. The image has been cropped to fit the dimensions of the cover.

2. The illustration of the month of August used on the back cover is from the French Gothic illuminated manuscript *Les Très Riches Heures du duc de Berry* by the Limbourg Brothers, Jean Colombe, and an intermediate painter whose name is lost to history. It is in the public domain because its copyright has expired.

3. The box graphic used on the first page is from a 1916 pamphlet entitled "Divorce versus Democracy" authored by G. K. Chesterton, originally published in London by the Society of St. Peter and St. Paul. It is in the public domain in the US because it was published prior to 1923, and is in the public domain in all countries (including the country of origin) in which the copyright time is the author's life plus 70 years or less.

4. The graphic design for the section pages in this book is from a design originally created for a pharmacy label. It is courtesy of Wellcome Images (ICV No 11073, photo V0010813), and is used here under CC BY-SA 4.0.

5. The trade card "The Moon of Sturgeon August" by P. D. Beckwith was created circa 1909, and is in the public domain because its

copyright has expired. It is from the Victorian Trade Cards Collection at Miami University Libraries (accession no. 1200).

6. The photograph of the first US Air Force Academy class is in the public domain as a work taken by an employee of the US government as part of that person's official duties.

7. The 2009 photograph of new US Air Force Academy cadets in their first formation was taken for US Air Force Public Affairs by Mike Kaplan. It is in the public domain as a work taken by an employee of the US government as part of that person's official duties.

8. The 2009 photograph of the graduation of the US Air Force Academy Class of 2009 was taken for Defense News Service by Dennis Rogers. It is in the public domain as a work taken by an employee of the US government as part of that person's official duties.

9. The 1914 photograph of Ishi by Saxton T. Pope is in the public domain because its copyright has expired.

10. The 1978 photograph of the Goodyear Blimp is copyright © Tequask, and is used here under CC BY-SA 4.0.

11. The August 29, 1965, photograph of the Gemini V astronauts is in the public domain as a work created solely by NASA (photo ID GPN-2000-001494).

12. The October 1963 photograph of The Beatles at Hötorgscity, Stockholm is in the public domain in Sweden, it country of origin, because it was a journalistic work created before 1969. It is in the public domain in the United States because it was published in the US between 1923 and 1963 and although there may or may not have been a copyright notice, the copyright was not renewed.

13. The 1944 publicity photograph of Ingrid Bergman in *Gaslight* is in the public domain because it was first published in the United States between 1923 and 1977 without a copyright notice. Traditionally, publicity photographs are not copyrighted because of the way in which they are intended to be used.

14. The 1697 portrait of John Locke by Sir Godfrey Kneller is in the State Hermitage Museum, St. Petersburg, Russia. It is in the public domain because its copyright has expired.

15. The cover of the January 9, 1933, issue of *Time* magazine is in the public domain because it was published in the United States between 1923 and 1963, and although it was originally copyrighted, the copyright was not renewed. *Time* only began regularly renewing copyrights as of the July 6, 1936, issue.

16. The 1986 photograph of James Brady by William Fitz-Patrick is in the public domain as a work created by an employee of the US government as part of that person's official duties.

17. The 2009 official Senate portrait photograph of John McCain is in the public domain as a work created by an employee of the US government as part of that person's official duties.

18. The 1977 publicity photograph from *The Jacksons* is in the public domain because it was first published in the United States between 1923 and 1977 without a copyright notice.

19. The circa 1947 photograph of Charlie Parker is from the William P. Gottlieb Collection at the Library of Congress (digital ID gottlieb. 06941). In accordance with the wishes of William Gottlieb, the photographs in this collection entered into the public domain on February 16, 2010.

20. The 1986 publicity photograph of Elliott Gould in *Together We Stand* is in the public domain because it was first published in the United States between 1923 and 1977 without a copyright notice.

21. The 2010 photograph of Roy Oswalt is copyright © D. B. King, and is used here under CC BY-SA 2.0.

22. The 1968 photograph of Bob Beamon is courtesy Dutch National Archives (ANEFO), The Hague, identification number 922-2039. It is used here under CC BY-SA 3.0 Netherlands.

23. The 1961 publicity photograph of Lee Marvin in *The Twilight Zone* is in the public domain because it was first published in the United States between 1923 and 1977 without a copyright notice.

24. The 1924 photograph of Leopold and Loeb was taken by Georg Pahl for Aktuelle-Bilder-Centrale (Bild 102-00652), and has been made available by the German Federal Archive (Bundesarchiv) under CC BY-SA 3.0 Germany.

25. The caricature of William Spooner by Leslie Ward was first published in *Vanity Fair*, April 21, 1898, issue. It is in the public domain because its copyright has expired.

26. The 1942 publicity photograph from *Sherlock Holmes and the Voice of Terror* is in the public domain because it was first published in the United States between 1923 and 1977 without a copyright notice.

27. The 1955 publicity photograph from *Make Room for Daddy/The Danny Thomas Show* is in the public domain because it was first published in the United States between 1923 and 1977 without a copyright notice.

28. The photograph of Brigham Young by Charles William Carter was taken between 1866 and 1877. It is in the public domain because its copyright has expired.

29. The 1870 photograph of Pierre Lallemant is in the public domain because its copyright has expired.

30. The 1753 book *A Short Treatise on the Game of Back-Gammon* by Edmond Hoyle is in the public domain because its copyright has expired.

31. The painting *Miner* by Boris Jeremejewitsch Wladimirskij is in the public domain in its home country of Ukraine because it was published before January 1, 1951, and the creator died before that date. It is in the public domain in the US because it was in the public domain in Ukraine prior to January 1, 1966, and no copyright was registered in the US.

32. The 2014 photo of the statue of Dhyan Chand is copyright by "Work2win," and is used here under CC BY-SA 3.0.

33. The 1944 photograph of Slovak mutineer forces of the 18th Anti Aircraft Artillery Battery is copyright by Pavel Pelech, who released the work for any purpose, providing the copyright holder is properly attributed.

34. The 2013 photograph of a chop suey restaurant sign is by Daderot, who released it into the public domain according to CC0 1.0 University Public Domain Dedication.

35. The 2011 photograph of a whiskey sour is copyrighted by "Jgilgamesh," and is used here under CC BY-SA 3.0.

36. The 1866 painting *Jar of Peaches* by Claude Monet is in the New Masters Gallery, Dresden, Germany, accession NM-2525-B-PS01. It is in the public domain because its copyright has expired.

37. The painting *The Feast of Herod* by Peter Paul Rubens was created prior to 1640, and is in the public domain because its copyright has expired. Collection of the Scottish National Gallery, accession no. NG2193.

38. The 1943 photograph of a Buffalo, New York, nursery school for children of working mothers was taken by Marjory Collins for the Office of War Information. It is in the public domain as a work created by an employee of the US federal government as part of that person's official duties. The original photo is in the collection of the Library of Congress, digital ID fsa.8d18633.

39. The 1860 advertisement for Pony Express riders is in the public domain because its copyright has expired.

40. The photograph of a tug-of-war competition at the 1904 St. Louis Olympic Games is from the book *The Olympic Games*, by Charles Lucas (St. Louis: Woodward and Tiernan, 1905). It is in the public domain because its copyright has expired.

41. The painting "August" is from the *Brevarium Grimani,* circa 1510, and is in the public domain because its copyright has expired.

42. The 1815 woodcut of a proposal is in the public domain because its copyright has expired.

43. The photograph of an emerald cut peridot was taken by Michelle Jo, who released it into the public domain in 2009.

44. The photograph of the Cup of the Ptolemies was taken by "Clio20" and is used here under CC BY-SA 3.0. The cup is in the collection of the Bibliothèque Nationale de France.

45. The 1886 paintings *Vase with Cornflowers and Poppies* by Vincent van Gogh are in the public domain because its copyright has expired.

46. The 1886 painting *Vase with Red Gladioli* by Vincent van Gogh is in the public domain because its copyright has expired.

47. The 1886 painting *Vase with Cornflowers and Poppies* by Vincent van Gogh is in the public domain because its copyright has expired.

48. The 1896 illustration *August* by Eugène Grasset is in the public domain because its copyright has expired.

49. The celestial sphere is from *Scenography of the Ptolemaic Cosmography,* by Johannes van Loon, based on Andreas Cellarius's *Harmonia Macrocosmica,* 1660. It is in the public domain because its copyright has expired.

50. The 1906 automobile calendar is by Edward Penfield, and is in the collection of the Library of Congress Prints and Photographs Division. It is in the public domain because its copyright has expired.

51. The 50-year perpetual calendar photograph is in the public domain.

52. The cartoon by John T. McCutcheon is from his 1905 collection *The Mysterious Stranger and Other Cartoons* by John T. McCutcheon. It is in the public domain because its copyright has expired.

53. The painting *August* by Joachim von Sandrart is in the public domain because its copyright has expired. The original can be found in the Staatsgalerie im Neuen Schloss, Schleißheim, Germany.

54. The painting *August* by Hans Thoma is from his book *Festkalender.* It is in the public domain because its copyright has expired.

License Description and Terms

Aside from material purely in the public domain, photographs and other material in this book are used under specific licenses permitting free use, usually with an attribution requirement. For full text and terms of these licenses, click or enter the appropriate links below. If you believe there is an error in the copyright status or attribution of any of these images, please email us.

- Creative Commons Attribution 2.0 Generic (CC-BY 2.0): http://creativecommons.org/licenses/by/2.0/deed.en
- Creative Commons Attribution-Share Alike 3.0 Generic (CC-BY-SA 3.0): http://creativecommons.org/licenses/by-sa/3.0/
- Creative Commons Attribution-Share Alike 2.5 Generic (CC-BY-SA 2.5): http://creativecommons.org/licenses/by-sa/2.5/deed.en
- Creative Commons Attribution-Share Alike 2.0 Generic (CC-BY-SA 2.0): http://creativecommons.org/licenses/by/2.0/deed.en
- Creative Commons Attribution-Share Alike 1.0 Generic (CC-BY-SA 1.0): http://creativecommons.org/licenses/by-sa/1.0/deed.en
- CC0 1.0 Universal (CC0 1.0) Public Domain Dedication (CC0 1.0) http://creativecommons.org/publicdomain/zero/1.0/deed.en
- GNU Free Documentation License (GFDL): http://en.wikipedia.org/wiki/Wikipedia:Text_of_the_GNU_Free_Documentation_License
- License Art Libre (Free Art License): http://artlibre.org

Timespinner
Press

August, by Joachim von Sandrart

Other Books from Timespinner Press

Timespinner
Press

The Story of a Special Day

Michael Dobson

A series of (eventually) 366 volumes covering everything that happened on your special day! Events, births, deaths, quotes, holidays, and much more. It's like a birthday card they'll never throw away!

US$7.95 print / US$2.99 ebook.

From Plassey to Pakistan

Humayun Mirza

The history of British Colonial India and the formation of Pakistan from the unique perspective of the son of Pakistan's first president and last of the royal line of Bengal, Bihar, and Orissa! This unique historical document tells the inside story of this distinguished family, including the detailed story of the coup that toppled his father from power!

US$27.95 print

A Whole New Navy: America's War in the Pacific

Miles Durr

The most comprehensive and detailed description of America's naval war in the Pacific ever—every battle, every ship, every task force and every task group from Pearl Harbor through the Japanese surrender! A must-have for the collection of every World War II buff!

US$29.95 print

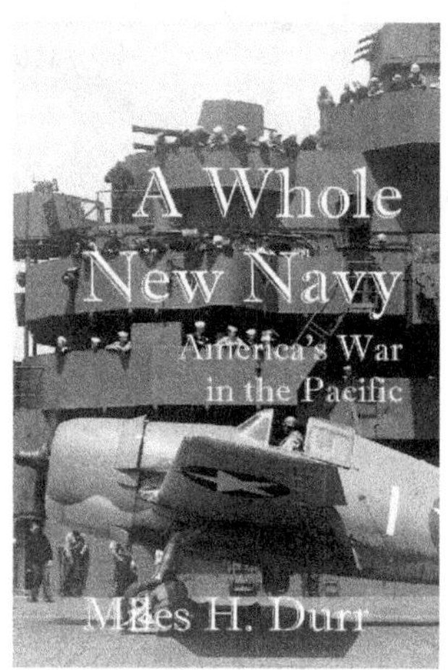

Improbable History: The Weird, the Obscure, and the Strangely Important

edited by Michael Dobson

From the birth of Western civilization to the rescue of Apollo 13, from the Leaning Tower of Pisa to Florence's Duomo, history has often turned on small, improbable details. Whatever happened to the ancient Samaritan people? Why did a fortuitous rainstorm allow the British to conquer India? How did an air raid in Italy lead to the development of chemotherapy? What happened when Albert Einstein met Adolf Hitler on the streets of Berlin? How did the Japanese manage to attack the US mainland using balloons? A cast of award-winning writers tackle some of the strangest tales in history!

US$19.95 print

The Letters of William Philip Schwartz 1842-1855

edited by John F. Schwartz

The 19th century soldier and adventurer William Philip Schwartz wrote a series of vivid and detailed letters chronicling his adventures in the Indian Wars, the Mexican-American War, the Gold Rush, and his term as Marine sergeant aboard the USS Constellation. A pioneer in photography, he took *the first known war photographs*. An unforgettable first-hand look into life in the 19th century!

US$17.95 print

Watergate Considered as an Organization Chart of Semi-Precious Stones (and other essays)

by Michael Dobson

In this light-hearted yet insightful tour through the Nixon White House, the Committee to Re-Elect the President, and the various investigative committees, you'll meet fascinating characters from Richard Nixon himself to such lieutenants as a G. Gordon Liddy and John Dean. You'll gain insights into the origin of the scandal, the motives of the players, and how the situation spiraled so badly out of control.

US$9.95 print/US$3.99 ebook

August, by Hans Thoma

www.ingramcontent.com/pod-product-compliance
Lightning Source LLC
Chambersburg PA
CBHW060749260726
48660CB00002B/543